The
Peaceful
Lotus

RP Minis™
Hachette Book Group
1290 Avenue of the Americas, New York, NY 10104
www.runningpress.com
@Running_Press

First Edition: April 2020

Published by RP Minis, an imprint of Perseus Books, LLC,
a subsidiary of Hachette Book Group, Inc. The RP Minis
name and logo is a trademark of the Hachette Book Group.

The publisher is not responsible for websites
(or their content) that are not owned by the publisher.

ISBN: 978-0-7624-9446-0

CONTENTS

INTRODUCTION:
THIS IS THE LOTUS FLOWER

Zen. Calm. Peace.
Purity. Birth. Grace.
Compassion. Serenity.
Resilience.
This is the Lotus flower.

The Lotus flower (*Nelumbo nucifera*) has become a universal symbol of peace, calm, serenity, and beauty. In *The Peaceful Lotus*, we'll go through why the Lotus flower is such a powerful talisman and what you'll be reminded of and inspired by when you see your own Lotus flower replica on your desk. Join us on this journey as we discover the meaning behind the wonder that is the Lotus flower.

Perhaps the most defining characteristic of the Lotus flower is that it grows in shallow, murky waters. Emerging from mud and dirt, a beautiful flower blooms atop the water. Lotus flowers are native to Asia and they flourish in warm climates. In fact, they are intolerant to cold weather. The flowers—and sometimes the leaves—bloom above the water, creating a beautiful visual of the Lotus floating gracefully atop the pond where it grows. Lotus flowers are open by day but close at night.

"Whenever you should
doubt your self-worth,
remember the Lotus flower.
Even though it plunges to
life from beneath the mud,
it does not allow the dirt
that surrounds it to affect
its growth or beauty."

— *Suzy Kassem*

THE LOTUS FLOWER
IN BUDDHISM.

"The secret of health for both mind and body is not to mourn for the past, worry about the future, or anticipate troubles, but to live in the present moment wisely and earnestly."

— *Buddha*

The Eight Auspicious Symbols of Buddhism

Buddhists consider the Lotus a sacred flower; it is one of the Eight Auspicious Symbols of Buddhism. Different Buddhist traditions order the eight symbols differently.

Conch Shell: Representing the deep melodic sound of dharma

Dharmachakra: Representing Gautama Buddha and the teaching of Dharma

Endless Knot: Representing the unity of everything; all is one

Golden Fish: Representing happiness, fearlessness, and freedom

Jeweled Parasol: Representing protection from harmful forces

Lotus Flower: Representing the purity of body, speech, and mind

Treasure Vase: Representing longevity, wealth, prosperity, and health

Victory Banner: Representing victory over obstacles on the path to enlightenment

Lotus Flower Symbolism

The Lotus flower represents many things to Buddhists, including good fortune, purity, and faithfulness. Because it is planted in muck and gloomy waters but rises to the surface a beautiful flower, the Lotus is a symbol for overcoming obstacles and rising strong and pure.

Lotus flowers are often used as a reminder that one must go

through the bad times in life to enjoy and appreciate the good. Suffering is an inevitable part of the human existence—a Lotus flower is widely used as a symbol of the beauty and happiness that can come from even the darkest places.

Meaning of Lotus Flower Colors

When it comes to the colors of its petals, there are many variations of the Lotus flower. The most common Lotus, the image that most people think of when they hear its name, is a pink flower. However, they can also bloom blue, red, purple, white, or gold. Different color flowers represent different meanings in Buddhism.

Red: Compassion and love

Pink: The history of Buddha

Purple: Spiritual awakening

White: Purity of mind and spirit

Blue: Logic and common sense

Gold: Achievement of enlightenment

Lotus at Different Stages of Growth

Like the color of the petal, each stage of growth of the Lotus flower has a different meaning to Buddhists. A closed lotus represents the time when a new Buddhist follower is practicing but has not yet reached enlightenment. A Lotus flower that is opened and in bloom represents the manifestation of that enlightenment.

Lotus Flower and a Sense of Calm

When water or mud falls on to the petals of the Lotus, it simply slides off and the flower remains unaffected. Like the powerful representation of the flower emerging from the muck, this quality is also cited often as a reminder to be like the Lotus, unperturbed by life's little disturbances. The Lotus remains at peace throughout the storm.

"You cannot grow Lotus flowers on marble. You have to grow them on the mud. Without mud you cannot have Lotus flowers. Without suffering, you have no way to learn how to be understanding and compassionate."

— *Thich Nhat Hanh*

Fertility and Rebirth

A Lotus flower is also a symbol of fertility in Hindu culture, and it represents rebirth in Buddhism. Rebirth can refer to overcoming challenges and making a big change in life, or actual birth, rebirth, or reincarnation. A Lotus flower talisman is sometimes given to a woman experiencing trouble getting pregnant as a good luck charm.

THE LOTUS
FLOWER IN YOGA

"Yoga means addition—
addition of energy, strength,
and beauty to body, mind
and soul."

—*Amit Ray*

In yoga, the energy centers throughout one's body are called chakras. Lotus flowers, with varying number of petals, are used to refer to each chakra.

The *crown chakra*, which is the seventh energy center located at one's head, is represented by a thousand-petaled Lotus, indicating full enlightenment.

Lotus Pose

There is also a pose in yoga called *Pasmasana*, better known as the Lotus pose. When one is seated in Lotus pose, their legs are crossed with the tops of their feet resting on either thigh, soles facing upward. In this way, the human body mimics the Lotus flower, with splayed, open petals facing the sun. Lotus pose is a common and simple yoga pose, but is a powerful one, too, offering a sense of simultaneous grounding and energy.

Lotus pose is a hip and heart opener, giving the yogi a feeling of opening and acceptance, as well as calm groundedness and strength— just like its namesake flower.

The Shiva Sahmita, a sanskirt text on yoga, says: "When the yogi seated in the Lotus posture leaves the ground and remains firm in the air, he should know that he has attained mastery over that life-breath which destroys the darkness of the world." A powerful pose, to say the least!

Besides the spiritual and mental benefits, the Lotus pose can also be extremely beneficial from a medical and pain-eradication standpoint. Practicing the Lotus pose is said to ease menstrual pain and sciatica, stretch the ankles and knees, and help create balance in the metabolic system.

"The body is your temple.
Keep it pure and clean
for the soul to reside in."

—B. K. S. Iyengar

THE LOTUS FLOWER
AND THE SUN

"No sun outlasts
its sunset, but will
rise again and bring
the dawn."

—*Maya Angelou*

Egyptians associated the Lotus flower with the sun, noting the similarity between the flower closing at night and opening in the morning and the disappearance of the sun at night, only to return in the morning. The Lotus symbolized the sun and creation in ancient Egyptian hieroglyphics. Lotus flowers are thought of as shining and bright, rising from the dark to illuminate the day.

LET YOUR LOTUS SHINE

Strength. Beauty.
Balance. Light. Renewed.
Open. Loving. Grounded.
This is the Lotus flower.

Your Desktop Lotus

It's never been easier to evoke the calm and peace of the Lotus flower than with this beautiful replica, which creates a tranquil, serene setting with its cool, soothing glow and the gentle sound of babbling water. Simply insert two double-A batteries, flip the switch on the underside of the pond to "ON," and place the Lotus flower somewhere within your line of sight. If you're able, dim the lights to really experience the

changing colors of the flower's
glow, allowing yourself to focus
only on the present moment.
Allow your mind to find calm.
As you go through your day, gaze
upon this talisman and remember
the Lotus flower and all of its
lessons. When stress or hard times
arise, be like the Lotus—calm,
strong, rising from the mud to
shine brightly in the sun.

"Just like the Lotus,
we too have the ability to
rise from the mud, bloom
out of the darkness, and
radiate into the world."

— *Unknown*

This book has been bound using
handcraft methods and
Smyth-sewn to ensure durability.

The box and interior were
designed by Christopher Eads.

The text was written by
Mollie Thomas.